Some Glad Morning

Some Glad Morning

IRENE FORD-SMITH

Foreword by Eric J. Smith

VMH™ Publishing
Copyright © 2021 by Irene Ford-Smith

VMH ™ Publishing
3355 Lenox Rd. NE Suite 750
Atlanta, GA 30326
www.vmhpublishing.com

The publisher is not responsible for websites, or social media pages (or their content) related to this publication, that are not owned by the publisher. Quantity sales. Special discounts are available on quantity purchases by corporations, associations, and others. For details, contact the publisher via email at: info@vmhpublishing.com
Irene Ford-Smith Cover Photography: Lindria Dockett Photography
Irene Ford-Smith Make-Up Artist: Jennifer Thorpe Beauty

Hardback ISBN: 978-1-947928-96-1
Paperback ISBN: 978-1-947928-98-5
Ebook ISBN: 978-1-7378324-9-2
Library of Congress Control Number:

Published in United States of America
10 9 8 7 6 5 4 3 2 1

I am thankful to my husband, Melvin Smith, who provides me the space and time to do the myriad of things I enjoy. I am thankful to my three sons, Melvin Jr., Jason, and Eric who are always supportive. My grandchildren biological and otherwise—Chase, Eric, Jason, Justin, Makaila, Richard, Unique, Lyric, Elijah, and Shan—who bring me such joy. I am forever thankful to Rasheda, Sanetra, Valencia, Malvolia, Gloria, Kimberly, and Brenda who always give me a listening ear. Without the entire team of volunteers who serve with me during the homegoing services, I would not be able to stand. Some of these volunteers are Deacon Walter J. Harvey, Deacon Robert Dunlap, Deacon William (Bill) Barnes, Minister James Durham, Alease Cookie Montgomery, the usher and repast volunteers, Marcus Young, Pamela Harris and Vickie Hunter.

This book would not be possible without the assignment given to me by Dr. Delman L. Coates, my pastor, and the vote of confidence from the members of Mt. Ennon Baptist Church.

Thank you, Lord Jesus for this assignment!

Content

Foreword

I'd like to use this space to honor my mother, the author of this book. In both her motherhood and her ministry, Mom has committed herself to teaching the life-lessons that have brought her joy: always seek God first; difficult times do not define a person; life is about perspective; and serving God means serving others. While my mother has given these lessons through lectures to her children, sermons to her church, and now through this book, her actions infuse her words with real power.

Her whole life long, my mother has had a deep desire to serve God. However, for some time, she was unable to serve in the capacity she most desired: that of a minister. Along with other women, Mom courageously voiced what she believed women were capable of within the church. She demonstrated that capability by serving individuals and organizing service efforts within the church community. She pursued her seminary education to hone her abilities and prepare for ministry service. I remember watching and listening to her first sermon. I didn't understand her impact at the time, but she was paving the way for other women in ministry.

And she did all of this while raising me and my brothers with immense love and care. Aside from securing a good education for us, she helped us cultivate our spirituality, pursue our interests, and build strong relationships with friends and family. Through her example, she taught us how to serve others and give back to the church. She pushed us beyond some of our shortsighted thoughts and desires, and when we did make mistakes, she navigated the situations with patience and love.

Though my mother's name, Irene, may have been given to her by her biological parents, it was selected by her Heavenly Father. The Greek translation of Irene is peace. The Arabic translation is calmness and contentment. Irene Ford-Smith embodies these definitions and offers them to you in her novel. You will smile and laugh but may also cry and even experience anger. In the service of God and others, leaders sometimes have to put their own thoughts and feelings aside. My hope is that by the end of this novel you will understand that these moments of grief and frustration are essential to experiencing peace and joy.

Irene, on behalf of the many members of your tribe, thank you for being such an inspiration. Your life has touched ours, and we are forever changed for the better.

On behalf of your sons, thank you for the invaluable lessons which allow us to take on the world. Your unconditional love strengthens us every day.

I love you and will always admire your spirit, strength, and grace.

Eric J. Smith

Introduction

I am not sure how I became the eulogist for death, but God decided this was my path.

In the beginning, as a young mother of two toddlers, I volunteered to serve in the Church Nursery with the babies. It was the perfect place for me. As my children grew, I changed ministry with them and volunteered to serve in the Children Choir with Brother and Sister Steven & Carrie Young. They decided to begin a choir for the younger children (ages three to five) since they could not be a part of the older choir. Of course, they needed a director, and I was volunteered to lead. Do I know anything about directing younger children, much less teaching them? The answer "No!"

God certainly calls the unprepared and then performs the work inside you to guide and direct. As the years passed, I received my call to the ministry. A call I refused to accept, but God moves in ways we can never fully understand. I was not fully accepted into the ministry because I was a woman, but GOD! Today, I am an ordained minister of the Gospel where I bear the responsibility and the joy of ministering to those who are experiencing grief and sorrow.

I write this book to share my memoirs, while some experiences will make you smile, and others may make you cry. My prayer is these writings will bring comfort, give hope, and be a source of encouragement. For my sisters in the ministry, I pray you will be bolstered and continue to walk in your calling. And for my brothers, I pray from this day forward you will give thought to your words and actions towards the women in ministry.

I am especially thankful to the church secretary, the dedicated ushers, the assigned deacons, the Media, Music & Arts Ministry, the Administrative Team, the Repast Team, the greeters, and Minister James Durham who often serves with me. We are a united team, and it shows from the many compliments we receive. When a family is attending the home going service, they have no idea we have already been to the church two or more times in one week and four to six times in one month serving other families. Each time we meet a family it is as if they are our first, and we give them our very best.

As a team we have learned so much; each member knows exactly how to operate and how to meet the needs of the families, friends, and others who come to the service. I am eternally grateful to my Pastor, Dr. Delman L. Coates, and the Mt. Ennon Church family for their confidence in my calling and the support they always give.

Jeremiah 29:11 "For I know the plans I have for you," declares the LORD, "plans to prosper you and not to harm you, plans to give you hope and a future."

CHAPTER

1

The Beginning

For many years I simply attended homegoing services; I peered in while others ministered to the emotional and spiritual needs of the parishioners. I was never asked to do anything, and I never requested. As the years went by, I was asked to read scripture or offer a prayer which was sufficient for me.

At the right season, when God determined I was ready, I traveled to a hospital to minister to a young mother whose infant was killed in a horrific car accident. I remember being at the hospital praying to God for guidance on what to say. No one had ever prepared me for this burden of grief. As the funeral director arrived, he had the tiny casket draped in a white cloth tucked under his arm. Everyone at the hospital was prepared to assist this young mother in saying goodnight for a season to her beautiful infant son. When the casket was opened, the baby looked like a beautiful porcelain doll. The mother began to wail. I offered a prayer for her, spoke words of hope, and consoled her as an older mother to a younger one, a mother to a daughter, a minister to a hurting child of God. My heart broke, and I thank God for holding my tears until I got to my car.

My initiation into homegoing services began. Death teaches you the importance of relationships, the importance of expressing your love to family, friends, and others. It teaches the importance of forgiveness and of creating beautiful memories. Walking away from the hospital, I learned life is fleeting. This mother was leaving church on her way home when this terrible car accident occurred, and her life changed forever.

Psalms 23:4 Yea, though I walk through the valley of the shadow of death, I will fear no evil: for thou *art* with me; thy rod and thy staff they comfort me.

❄ ❄ ❄

CHAPTER

2

Seared in My Heart

The next homegoing service, which remains with me as if just occurred and is seared in my heart forever, was a little five-year-old girl who was losing her battle to cancer and gaining her heavenly wings. She was so brave. I first took notice of her when she came to church with a scarf wrapped around her head. I later discovered she was going through chemo which had taken her hair but not her spirit. She was a beautiful, brown-skinned little girl with a big personality and the older sister to her little brother. How they loved each other! They were extremely

11

close, and his big sister looked after him. I visited this tiny beauty in her last days at the children's hospital.

As I spoke with her, I recalled she loved butterflies, so I told her God was going to make her butterfly. That was our last conversation. I remember the day of the service so well. Even today, I sigh and wipe tears from my eyes when I recall her little brother's face as he went from playing at the service to the realization that his sister was dead and would not be with him anymore. He began to look around the room; he saw the people dressed in suits, the casket, the choir, and the reality that his sister's voice was now quiet.

Suddenly, he began to call out her name, begging her to wake up, wake up. I must pause even now and take a deep breath for it is still painful. There was not a dry eye in the chapel. His mother found it difficult to console him as she was going through her own grief. The father held him and consoled him until he stopped calling for his sister to wake up and play with him. Homegoing services are difficult; they are heartbreaking and a gentle reminder to hold your children, your nieces, your nephews a little tighter.

I have visited the children's hospital to visit with many parents of toddlers, infants, and school-age children. It is always a tremendous wrenching of the heart, especially being a mother and grandmother, to be surrounded by so many very ill children. However, what I have learned from visiting these very young patients is that they are resilient. As I have visited and held newborns in the prenatal unit, my prayer has remained "God you can do all things but fail." He still heals, strengthens, and restores.

I have many vivid memories of seeing these babies, but I recall an infant who had undergone many surgeries to preserve his life. It is something, seeing a newborn with tubes, needles, and marks of surgery on his chest. I didn't have the luxury of turning away or walking out of the room.

My mission from God is to speak words of hope, encouragement, and trust in God no matter the situation because I still trust God for the miraculous. As I looked at the infant laying on his back with tubes and signs of major surgery on his small chest, my heart hurt. I spoke with the mother and father, and they expressed their hopes for the sweet baby's recovery, trusting for the best. I too prayed, believing.

No sense praying if you are not believing, and I was believing. The baby lost the battle, and God called him home. What about your prayers? God's will for this young infant was to call the child back into His loving arms. With no more surgeries, no more prodding, and no more tubes, this infant was at rest. My responsibility then shifted to reminding the parents of God's love. I still remember praying to God to give me a word of encouragement for these young parents to hold them together, bind them with His love, and keep them from fighting each other out of grief.

I recall another homegoing service where it was revealed that the father was married to another woman (not legally). He led his wife, the mother of the baby, to believe he was working out of state while living less than 25 miles away with another woman he had married. The wife came earlier and left; the other wife (not legal) remained for a very awkward service.

Just recently, I eulogized three babies and my heart ached for their parents. I watched them place their small caskets on a horse-drawn carriage. The beauty of it. The immense sadness. I am asked, "Do you remember all the funerals you do?" Some I will never forget, but I try to walk away from each with a life lesson that I can implement and share with others.

Then there was the homegoing service for an older woman where *I* didn't preach. Yet so many souls were surrendered to Christ on that day. As I stood to preach, I began to pray aloud, and God's voice spoke to me. God said there is a man here who has been praying for me to intervene in his life, and today I want him to know I have heard his cry. I was praying out loud and having a private conversation with God, "are you sure, I have never done anything like this before." I did not want to end the prayer, but I did. Just as the Spirit directed me, I said "I have never done anything like this before, but while I was praying, God spoke to me and told me there is a man here who has been praying, and you needed to know today is the day God has heard your prayer." I kept talking, and before I finished, men began crying, standing, and coming to the front of the church. I kept on speaking what the Holy Spirit was saying while the Minister of Music continued to play. It was about an hour of men crying, falling to the ground, and surrendering themselves to the Lord. The men who came forward were both young and old, all desiring a closer walk, all releasing themselves to freely worship. It was a defining moment. I never preached the eulogy, God did!

Lastly, deaths by accidents are seared in my heart because they are extremely difficult for family members and close friends. I remember visiting a family who's loved one had been killed in an accident. Like so many others, the family members' minds had captured the moment they last spoke with the deceased—those final words—and the undeniable shock they felt when informed of the death. As I have talked with so many whose loved ones have died in unexpected accidents, the greatest difficulty they experience is not being able to express their love. I always prepare myself to hear and bear the tremendous hurt expressed by the family. I have learned it is better to be a good listener versus interjecting "those familiar quotes." As I prepare to leave their presence, I pray for their peace, for the release of their pain, and their protection.

Psalm 116:1-2 I love the Lord, for He heard my voice; He heard my cry for mercy. [2]Because He turned His ear to me, I will call on Him as long as I live.

❄ ❄ ❄

CHAPTER

3

The Intersection

I have preached many eulogies and each service is different. I accepted my call to the ministry at a time in which women were not readily accepted. Even my pastor did not receive women in the ministry. He made it very clear to me that he would give me a letter to go to another church. I thanked him, telling him that God had not told me to leave. But there were times when I wanted to leave because it was difficult. I am thankful for the experience; it taught me how to trust in God no matter how I was treated. I am forever grateful to Gloria Harris who comforted me when my tears would not stop falling as I was trying to remain

17

strong. Finally, my pastor received me and became a strong supporter. However, when we would travel with him to preach, I was always asked to sit in the pew. I knew it was God who had changed his heart and perspective.

I learned man does not validate my calling, God does. Thus, I have learned how to own the pulpit when I am preaching. Although the statement sounds conceited, it is not. What I am saying is I have learned that when I stand to preach God is using me for his glory. So, like the Apostle Paul told Timothy, "Don't be timid."

I am a woman who, often, is overlooked initially and never thought to be the eulogist. So, the men on the team are acknowledged initially as the ones doing the eulogy. Once I am introduced as the person responsible for homegoing service, the very next question is "Will the pastor be here?" My response is "No," but I will certainly let him know you asked about him. I can see they are assessing me, unsure if I can handle the responsibility. What they do not know is the sheer number of eulogies I have preached.

When the service is over, I am congratulated for peaching (go figure). I have learned not to preach for applause, because often it gets quiet. I have learned people are listening and connecting to what I am saying. Yes, it is good to hear an "Amen," but it is better to preach "what thus saith the Lord." I do not ever want to find myself preaching to please anyone other than God. If you are patient, the Holy Spirit will give you the right word of encouragement for every family.

Some ask, "Do you ever recycle your sermons?" The answer is "no." I will reuse a Scripture, but the Holy Spirit always takes me in a different direction.

Homegoing services are outreach to the lost, to those who may be searching for a church home and/or desire a relationship with Jesus the Christ.

When I feel insufficient, I am reminded of my pastor's confidence in me, and I just smile. He trusts me with this awesome responsibility, he believes I can do it, and I can do it! I know without a doubt that God has called me to this ministry. Over and over, He has proven it to me and used me for His will. God always provides!

Colossians 4:6 Let your conversation be always full of grace, seasoned with salt, so that you may know how to answer everyone.

CHAPTER

4

The Unexpected

I received a call from the church asking me to go to a hospital in Washington, DC, to visit with a family whose children had been involved in a deadly accident. One of the young adult children had died, and the other was in the intensive care unit of a hospital in Washington, DC. I had never met the family, and when I arrived, I had no way of identifying the family. I went to the ICU phone and gave them the name of the patient and my identity as a minister.

As I went to the bedside, the young person was unconscious, and I prayed for healing. The mother came in and identified herself, and I went back to the family room to speak with them about the homegoing arrangements. Over the course of several days, the arrangements were finalized. The day before the service, the other child died. I was completely devasted because I understood the weight of grief and sorrow this mother was experiencing.

On the day of the service, I preached a sermon for both young people whose futures were so bright. I had to meditate, seeking the Lord, asking Him to give me the strength to minister to the family. The family members were a mix of both Christian and Muslim and had traveled a long distance for the service. Our team of ushers, deacons, and preachers moved gently amongst them, making them feel welcomed with the realization that some did not understand English or our customs. However, they did feel the love of the church. Both young people were outstanding students, stunningly beautiful, and well-loved by so many friends, and of course, their family. God always prepares you to stand!

I cannot write this book without mentioning Rev Dr. Allen Stanley such an awesome man of God. He celebrated a wonderful birthday, and within a few days, God called him home. I know for certainty "Doc" was ready to see Jesus and his beloved wife. However, it was not expected as his mind was sharp, and it just didn't seem like he would transition so quickly after his birthday. He loved God and oftentimes tears would fall from his eyes when we talked about heaven.

> **Romans 11:33-36** Oh, the depth of the riches of the wisdom and knowledge of God! How unsearchable his judgments, and his paths beyond tracing out!
>
> [34] "Who has known the mind of the Lord? Or who has been his counselor?"
>
> [35] "Who has ever given to God, that God should repay them?"
>
> [36] For from him and through him and for him are all things. To him be the glory forever! Amen.

Meeting People Where They Are

I met a man who was afraid of dying. The prognosis was not good. As we talked, he began to share his fear of dying. He wept. I held the man as if he were a young child and allowed him to cry. As I held him, I prayed and ask the Lord to give me the words to give him peace even amid a diagnosis of death. What could I offer him? The Spirit began to speak, and I shared with him Revelation 21. It is a powerful passage of scripture with the words so graphic you can almost reach out and touch heaven. I was there when he transitioned to Jesus, and I prayed with the family. At the hospital bed, I shared 1 Thessalonians chapter 4 with this man and his family. I hoped it would settle his spirit as he transitioned from earth to glory by reminding him of his eternal life. I hoped it would encourage the family by reminding them this was not the end. We have a home in glory, and Jesus will meet us there. I knew the man was okay for he had made his peace and accepted Jesus as his Savior. On the day of his service, God gave me a word of celebration to preach.

Very early in my ministry, I visited an elderly woman who was dying. She said to me "come on honey, do what you have come to do. I am on my way home once I get things right with my children." Some days later, she had closed her eyes and went on to glory with her work finished. What an awesome remembrance!

There are so many people I have visited who later succumbed to their illness. One such person was a faithful member of our church. Every time I left her bedside, I repeated "I love you; I love you!" She shouted back "I love you too!" Her voice is quiet, but I still hear her retort in my heart: "I love you." Yes, the preacher cries!

At one point, I became despondent about visiting people in the hospital, especially when I could see death on patients. No, I don't know how to explain it! I cried out to the Lord, saying "I don't want to go and how do I pray for healing when I see death?" Of course, the Lord I serve (and hopefully you serve) never slumbers nor sleeps, and He always has an answer. He reminded me of my responsibility to pray for the sick and conclude my prayers with "God's will be done." Yes, I pray fervently, asking for the person to be healed and restored, but I also pray "Lord, if it be your will, call them home gently into your peace." It may not be what the family wants to hear, but there is another set of ears listening, and I can never forget the person lying in the bed.

On the opposite end of the spectrum, I met a young woman who faced death without fear but with faith and trust in God. She had been fighting cancer for many years and the doctor's prognosis was that there was nothing else they could do. When I visited, she talked about sharing this prognosis with her family, her children, and extended family. She was the most gracious woman I have ever met. As I sat there talking, I began to ask myself if I would be so composed after hearing my death was imminent. The doctor told her about two weeks, but in our conversation, we both agreed only God knew the number of her days. I looked forward to visiting her in the hospital because every time she met me with her beautiful smile and gentle spirit.

Each time I left the room, I cried, unsure if that would be my last earthly visit. God called her home, and her death has changed me forever. I cry just thinking of this mother of two children with her beautiful, young spirit. She closed her eyes full of faith that Jesus was keeping her, holding her, and providing for her. And YES, our Savior never comes short of his promises.

John 8:51 Truly, truly I say to you if anyone keeps my word, he will never see death or taste death.

6

What to Say and What Not to Say

I still can hear the inconsolable mother wailing from her belly, crying out for her child. I pause when I begin to relive these moments. My heart breaks into a million pieces and tears fall. Nothing could prepare me to hear a mother wailing for her child. As a mom and grandmother, I know the love we have for our children. I pray a lot, asking the Lord to give me the right words to comfort. I pray that in my prayers I may stand by and minister to the bereaved—a mother, father, husband, and wife. As I rose to speak, I acknowledged this mother's pain and gently reminded her of where she would find the strength needed.

Two mothers will forever remain in my spirit. One could not move away from the casket and continued to gently pat the chest of her son while crying out for him. God help me! The other was a mother who had to be carried away from the casket as her grief overwhelmed her heart. God help me! These events sear my soul and remind me to never take a eulogy for granted, to never mount the pulpit unprepared, and to seek God's guidance before I stand.

I have learned that there are several phrases or expressions I should avoid. In my sermon, I preach heaven, but in a one-on-one conversation, I try to avoid saying "your loved one is in a better place." Of course, at the end of the day, the person knows this truth, but it is not something they want to hear at the time. I've learned not to ask, "how you are doing?" but "how are you coping?"

There are times when I feel the burden of responsibility in the pastoral position at homegoing services. One time, a preacher brought two harmonicas to a homegoing service for a young student who had died unexpectedly. The preacher began to play the instruments while doing a jig. I sat on the edge of my chair in utter disgust. This man was making a mockery of the moment, and I had to restrain myself from going up to the pulpit and snatching him down. After he finished, it was my pastoral responsibility to go up and offer words of comfort and strength to the family and friends who had gathered.

The eulogy is not always the place to reveal everything you think you know about a family relation. Just preach the word of God and the other information may be confided to the family later in a private setting.

I have learned to always remember that the family has invited coworkers and others to the service, and it is not the place to air faults. God can provide other ways to address issues.

God has taught me to practice patience and grace because everyone reacts and interacts differently.

Isaiah 51:16 I have put my words in your mouth and covered you with the shadow of my hand— I who set the heavens in place, who laid the foundations of the earth, and who say to Zion, 'You are my people.'

The Viewing: It's Possible to be Cussed Out

The viewing is the time set aside for the family and friends to say their final goodbyes. It is difficult for both family and friends. At the coffin, women, men, and children become overwhelmed with the finality of what has occurred. Some people who come to the church for homegoing services may have never set foot in a church before and may know very little about protocol. It was necessary to advise the team to not approach attendees about attire that could be considered disrespectful (i.e., tight and skimpy clothing or men wearing their hats in the church).

People come to homegoing services believing that they are dressed appropriately. It is imperative to receive everybody in love and to not impose our biased, personal thoughts on others. My pastor, Dr. Delman Coates, reminds us that people may not remember the message, but they will recall the reception, so don't give your company "a burnt biscuit." The only time we may say something is if low-hanging pants are exposing someone's underwear; otherwise, we are mum. We understand the homegoing service is an outreach opportunity to invite attendees to surrender their lives to Christ and come back for fellowship.

Sometimes we notice issues prior to the viewing. Perhaps the casket is not sized properly for the person, or there is no way of lifting the body up in the casket for better viewing, we notify the funeral directors of these issues. Other times, it appears that the body is sweating when it is thawing, sometimes an odor accompanies the body. We work alongside the funeral directors to ensure that all these issues are corrected before the family arrives. Before the family enters the sanctuary for the service, the entire Team is at work making sure that the room is accommodating for the family, we have discussed logistics and everyone is in place.

At our church, we generally wait for the family to arrive before we open the viewing. The family appreciates the opportunity to grieve privately. I remember a woman who came before the family had arrived and asked to see the deceased. She told us she was on her way to work and could not stay for the service. We informed her that unfortunately her request could not be granted. When the family arrived, the children of the deceased saw her and asked that she leave immediately. We later discovered this woman had an intimate relationship with the deceased. Yes, we were very happy we didn't allow her in before the family.

When the body of the deceased has been reconstructed and no one can touch the person during the viewing, people fight you the hardest. Some hurtful words are thrown at you and the homegoing service almost becomes a fight against you. These are the worst times for those who are serving—the funeral directors, the ushers, the ministers, and the family. There is always one person who is determined to touch the body even though they have been asked and told not to. The funeral directors, the ushers, the family, and the pastor all try to bring calm and dignity back into the service. We truly understand the hurt family and close friends experience when they can't even touch their loved one. During the viewing it is tense, and our goal is always to ensure the family, guest, and friends feel our love and concern.

Sometimes when the deceased person is young or well known, the lines for the viewing can be extremely long and if nothing is done, it would take hours for all the attendees to view the deceased. The team has learned ways to move the line at a faster pace, so everyone can say goodbye. However, those who come to the service once the family begins their final view, are requested to be seated. It is difficult to tell someone they are to late to view, it is not always received, it is difficult to give directions to persons who are emotionally charged they become very irate, ready to fight, and definitely tell you off.

We had a young man come to the viewing before the family identifying himself as the brother. We allowed him to go in and view. After some time, he became very defensive and inconsolable and refused to move from the coffin. Once the family arrived, we discovered the relationship was not quite like he said. Suddenly, he sat down and was very quiet. We had no further issues. What was his relationship? We never found out, but this was one of those instances where he was exhibiting violent behavior towards the ushers, deacons, and funeral directors.

In preparation for the viewing, we finalize cards to be read and identify persons whose names are in the program. Why? We had a family who had someone to read the cards, it took her 20 minutes. Other times, the family selects someone to read the acknowledgements who cannot read. Therefore, we decided it was best we have someone from the Team read the cards. We always try to make sure the soloist is present, we have instances where the soloist doesn't show up at all or arrive near the end of the service. We ensure that funerals start on time.

Occasionally fights occur during viewings. We are usually warned by the funeral directors of differences within the family, so we are on high alert. Yes, we have had to deal with families who refuse to sit by each other, and we are vigilant during the tribute since we don't know what either side might say.

If the deceased was murdered and the killer has not been captured, we always request security. Especially if it involves a young person murdered through gun violence. The team is always made aware of situations, so they are alert and mindful of responses from those who have come to the service.

Ushers usually experience pushback, cursing, and negative responses, and we have all learned not to respond. People who are hurting and grieving may act out of character, and our desire is for everyone to return safely home. We also want to create an unparalleled experience for those who come to the service. Without fail, the team has received so many great comments about their professionalism and their loving hospitality. We desire that everyone in attendance will meet Jesus in their interaction with the team.

Before we open the viewing to the public, we meet with the family. We greet them, introduce the team, and let them know what to expect from us. It is a great opportunity to answer any questions the family may have and make changes as requested, if possible.

The closing of the casket is often more than family members and friends can bear and may end with loud outbursts and wailing. At the closing of the casket, family members or close friends can become overwhelmed with grief and sorrow, often fainting, or collapsing. This sends everyone scurrying to get them up off the floor and into a chair. However, I have witnessed occasions in which family members collapsed, fainted and no one moved. Our Team will go over to assist getting them off the floor.

When the family is overwhelmed with grief, I have learned to move forward by reading scripture or requesting the choir or Minister of Music sing a song. This can bring order out of chaos and usher in the Spirit of God. I usually follow up with a prayer. Why? So that instead of the family becoming a spectacle, the family's emotional responses move the congregation to prayer.

Romans 8:38–39 For I am convinced that neither death nor life, neither angels nor demons, neither the present nor the future, nor any powers,

[39]neither height nor depth, nor anything else in all creation, will be able to separate us from the love of God that is in Christ Jesus our Lord.

❄ ❄ ❄

Family Ties That Do Not Bind

There are times when being the pastor of bereavement at a homegoing service places you in a family combat zone. Divided families refuse to sit with each other, are on the brink of fighting, and almost dare each other to act out. There is generally one group of family members seated on one side of the church and the other sitting on the other side.

There are numerous occasions during the service when there are obvious disagreements among the family. I remember one time, just as the service was getting started, those of us seated in the pulpit area noticed a conversation passing among family members. Persons walked out of the service in obvious anger, some walked in and out of the service, and some were even chased down to calm them. As a pastor, you are at the pulpit wondering "what is going on?" More times than I care to remember, the team has been required to leave the pulpit area meet outside the sanctuary with the family to resolve the internal issues without stopping the service. We usually must improvise and call on family members not listed on the program to come forward to give a tribute or sing a song to resolve hurt feelings.

I remember the time a brother and mother of the deceased showed up late. The service had started, and we had moved past the tributes. However, the brother wanted to speak and give his brother honor. As we sat listening to this older man give tribute to his brother, the direction of his remarks changed. He began to berate the deceased man's wife and express how much he hated her because she was no good and had isolated his brother from his family. At this point, everyone was looking at me and wondering what am was going to do. What could I do? Attempting to stop him would cause an even bigger scene. There was nothing left to do but let him finish and address the remarks at a more appropriate time.

On another occasion, the homegoing service of a father, the daughter refused to sit with her elderly mother, because the daughter felt her dad loved her more than anyone else.

Many hidden emotions are unveiled at homegoing service, so don't be surprised. Stay focused because the sermon is a powerful moment for healing to occur.

Matthew 18:21-22 Then Peter came and said to Him, "Lord, how often shall my brother sin against me and I forgive him? Up to seven times?"

²²Jesus said to him, "I do not say to you, up to seven times, but up to seventy times seven.

CHAPTER

9

Not Everyone Can Sing

The homegoing service presents an opportunity for a beautiful worship experience. The music can soothe heartache. Sometimes all it takes is listening to the lyrics of "Precious Lord," "God Promise Me a Home over There" by Jennifer Hudson, or "Take Me to the King" by Tasha Cobbs. Music can provide a personal resting place.

Music is essential at the homegoing service. When the Spirit is in the singer is doesn't matter whether they have an excellent voice or not. But that is the caveat!

For homegoing services, the family often selects the soloist, duets, violinist, or saxophone artist of their choice. We have our Minister of Music check in with them to find out exactly what they are going to sing or play. There have been occasions we had to say "no" because the selection was not appropriate for the church. It is a difficult conversation with the family especially if this was the person's favorite song. We simply remind them this is the church and not everything can be sung or played.

I have heard some beautiful voices and renditions of very popular worship songs. The voices heard at a homegoing service can range from operatic to deep bass, but they are almost always accompanied by the moving Spirit of God. Instrumentals are also powerful and often move the family and everyone present. You might be in trouble if you start hearing the congregation telling you "Take your time."

At the homegoing service, you have a captive audience, a stage, and a microphone, but not everyone can sing. Still, we've had some soloists with phenomenal voices. There was one young woman who riveted the congregation. Everyone sat up the moment she began to sing. She had the most beautiful unique voice I have ever heard. After the service, I asked her if she sang professionally, and she told me she did not. I told her that she needed to get a manager because her voice was beautiful. Her voice was so captivating and had such a fresh sound; all we could say was "wow!" But not everyone can sing.

There are other times when the choir or guest artist takes the service to a higher place in the Lord Jesus Christ. Now that's church talk—it simply means that the service is elevated because the Spirit of God is felt by everyone in the place. If you don't know what I am talking about, let me invite you to church. The family receives the blessing of peace through the music and Spirit of God moving within the hearts of everyone gathered. But not everyone can sing.

Yes, we had a young man come up and sing. It was not very long before we realized he could not sing. He jumped on the pulpit, threw his head back, and began to sing so bad. He thought he was at the Apollo Theater and the Church. Looking around the room everyone had the same expression, wondering whose idea was it to get this guy to sing! I sat wondering "how much longer before the song is over?" There are other times when the soloist sings a familiar song but is totally out of tune. You are praying for them to either find the tune or just end the song. On those occasions, I have learned to sit still with a straight face asking myself internally, how long Lord, how long!

Psalm 100:1-2 Shout for joy to the Lord, all the earth. [2]Worship the Lord with gladness; come before him with joyful songs.

CHAPTER

10

Two Minutes Is Not Always Two Minutes

I remember sitting while a woman read the cards. I closed my eyes and almost fell asleep for she read and read and read some more. I sat, wondering if she would ever finish, and finally, she finished. Perhaps this is the reason churches limit the reading of cards, letters, and proclamations.

Family members and friends are asked to give tributes, and some people do not understand what it means. People come with long manuscripts. Some start from the birth of the deceased and cover every milestone while others just talk about themselves. Finally, we found a way to at least keep some humor and not offend but gently tell the person that their time is up. When the speaker hears music playing softly, it is time to bring their tribute to an end. The louder the music, the more evident it is that their time is up. If we stand up, it is high time for them to sit down.

There is always the person who comes up to give a tribute and spends the entire time talking about themselves. There is the occasional person who comes up and says, "I don't know why the family asked me to speak, but I am honored." You want to ask the person: "Did you know you were coming to a homegoing service?" It is always a good idea to make notes to include the points you want to recall.

"Bootleg" is a term all preachers know. Bootleg occurs when preachers who have come as a guest go up to pray, read scripture, or give a tribute and end up preaching! I was taught whatever you are asked to do, just be obedient to the request. I remember a young man who came up to give tribute. He read a scripture, began to preach, opened the doors of the church, and got down on one knee at the end and prayed! The visiting preacher asked me, "what are you going to do Reverend Smith, has he done it all?" I said, "well he didn't preach what God gave me, so I am going up there and preach!" It's terrible when someone bootlegs a service because as preachers we know better. I believe this happens to me more often because I am a woman. Some of these men don't believe I am capable of preaching. I have learned that God called me to preach and equips me with the words, and I will not allow anyone to intimidate me!

2 Timothy 4:2 Preach the word; be prepared in season and out of season; correct, rebuke and encourage—with great patience and careful instruction.

Suicide and Murder

I have preached the eulogy for those have who committed suicide. I've even preached for those who have committed suicide after committing murder. These services keep me wrestling with God for the words to bring comfort to the family and friends.

The family of suicide victims may find themselves wrestling, wondering if they want the information disclosed. I met a brave mother who was determined to tell her son's story to help others. She came up to give tribute and the first thing she said was, "My son committed suicide. Let me share what he was experiencing so it may never happen to another person." He was a soldier, he was married, yet he felt bullied at his office by those around him. It doesn't matter whether it was true or not, for him it was real. So real that he took his life! Yes the pressure of being bullied is overwhelming and may led to suicide. I am prayerful changes have been made so no one else will suffer in silence but find a safe place for speaking out.

Another young man who was raised in the church experienced problems in his marriage and lost his way, killing his spouse and himself.

There was the mother who could not and would not accept the suicide of her child. In our conversations, it became clear there were some signs of depression. On the surface, a person may appear happy and successful but there are subtle warnings others had noticed.

I have learned to listen to the words being shared so I can facilitate open conversations which lead to healing. Sometimes we meet folks hiding behind a mask who are afraid to allow you to peer into their disfunction.

Depression is real and must not be dismissed but discussed with love and consideration. No, do not make the mistake of saying "just snap out of it." It is never easy; the person will prayer and professional care. Medication should never be looked at as a negative. Depression is like any other disease, and if it goes untreated it will get worse and may cost the life of a loved one. As family members, we must be alert to the words not spoken and the subtle changes in family members' and friends' personalities.

Friends and family members of suicide victims continually ask, "Could I have done more? Could I have changed the outcome? Could I have been more present? What did I miss?" All these questions are good, but once a person decides to take their life it may be impossible to stop them.

I have learned to be authentic about life experiences so others will be encouraged and recognize they can not only survive but thrive.

Psalm 34:18 The Lord is near to the brokenhearted and saves those who are crushed in spirit.

CHAPTER

12

COVID Services

When Covid hit the world, homegoing services did not stop. Services were held graveside and at the funeral homes with as little as 10 people including the directors and preacher. It has been a difficult season, especially since family members did not have the opportunity to spend the final moments with their loved ones.

It was during this season my brother became ill and underwent surgery. He was a diabetic, and the disease wreaked havoc on his body and prevented him from healing properly. He died, and it was time for me to digest all the lessons I had taught others. His service was graveside, with a limited number of attendees and social distancing. I could not touch his body. My heart ached.

I recalled doing my first Covid homegoing service at the graveside, and it was heartbreaking. There were only five family members present. They all stood six feet apart and wore masks and gloves. At the gravesite, there is no podium, no microphone, no choir. None of the familiar. The manuscript I was accustomed to using was no longer available. At the gravesite, I stood before the family preaching from the reserve God had deposited in me. Thereafter, while each service is always a little different, I was certainly more prepared. Preaching inside funeral homes to 10 people in masks who I had to speak to from afar and whom I could not hug was different. It was difficult to see wives or husbands burying their spouses with few family members present and with no human touch to comfort them.

Many services were held at the funeral home with a limited number of persons. Some required attendees to be fully masked throughout the service. It was important for me to learn how to speak clearly and loudly with a mask. I also had to remember that while I was speaking to a small audience within the walls of the funeral home, the service was being live streamed to hundreds. Additionally, there were time constraints; the funeral directors gave me between 30 minutes to an hour for the entire service.

The one-hour service becomes difficult when there are tributes to be given. Of course, some who stand to honor the deceased have given thought to what they want to say while others drift in their remarks. I have seen people come to the pulpit with manuscripts, and I've had to find a way to move the person along so that others have an opportunity to speak. You can never be sure of what people will say. Sometimes beautiful tributes are given while other times stagnant, ugly statements are made even in Covid.

With Covid, I usually do not have the opportunity to meet the family in person. Often, I don't receive the program until I arrive at the funeral home. I have eulogized so many individuals; some names are unfamiliar, but other times I have been overwhelmed because I recognize the person as someone from church or the community.

Through Covid, I have learned the importance of human touch, comfort, celebration, and of communicating love.

Matthew 18:20 For where two or three are gathered together in my name, there am I in the midst of them.

CHAPTER

13

The Cemetery

Y"ou are probably wondering what could possibly happen at the cemetery? Everything. I recall riding to the cemetery, with the beltway shut down. The beltway is a multi-lane highway (about four lanes). We had a police escort, only to realize we were traveling to the wrong cemetery. Yes, I chuckled.

When you travel to the cemetery, the funeral director is met by cemetery personnel who direct us to the gravesite. We arrived at the gravesite, and as we exited our cars, I began to raised voices. Even with the attendees present, a shouting match had broken out between the funeral director and the cemetery personnel at the back of the hearse. The cemetery staff offered advice to the funeral director which he had not solicited and which he negatively responded to. The argument just got louder and louder. Finally, they realized the spectacle they were making and settled themselves down.

At the gravesite, I saw a man drive over graves to pick up his wife, hitting two cars in the process. Everyone shouted, "Stop! STOP!" Once he finally came to a stop, we confronted him about his reckless driving, and he gave no answer. The representative from the cemetery told him to move his car. The man got back in his car and was about to drive over other graves but was stopped before he could. No one could figure out why he had decided to go around the bus in front of him and drive across graves. All he could say was he wanted to pick up his wife.

There are many insects at gravesites. I remember doing a committal with a bee was swarming around me. I gently swooshed it away, but it fell into my blouse. I wanted to scream but I stood very still, finished the committal, and then began walking very fast in the opposite direction, away from the family. I had to completely lift my blouse (yes, I exposed my bra) to get the bee out. And yes, I got stung several times.

I remember a woman at the gravesite of her husband. Though she was very stoic, it was evident that she loved her husband. Everyone had left the gravesite but me, and as I passed the woman, I heard her say, "Honey, I will see you in 100 years."

Going to the cemetery is the last opportunity during the service to give the family your very best. There are occasions when the family is so involved in taking pictures of the vault or looking for another family member's gravesite that they give little attention to the committal and to what you are saying. As the eulogist during the committal, you must remain focused no matter how many other conversations are going. I remember being at a committal when the funeral director told me to go ahead even though the family was not listening. I proceeded with the committal while the family took pictures of themselves and covered the vault with pictures of the deceased. No judgment. After all, the family has paid lots of money for the vault, and I cannot blame them for wanting to leave beautiful pictures of remembrance.

At military gravesites everything is precise and to the moment. You have about seven minutes to conduct the committal, so I try to make sure I use those seven minutes to comfort the family. The first time I went to the military gravesite, no one informed me how the 21-gun salute occurs. The rifle appears to be aimed at the inner chapel, the first time the soldier pulled the trigger I jumped so high. Oh, I was frightened! I was taken aback over the controversy of kneeling at the playing of the national anthem, I've noticed the soldier kneels every time to present the flag to family members. Kneeling is a sign of respect. It is an honor to escort the casket into the chapel and back out to the waiting hearse.

There are times when folks are crying, and you are not sure who is who. Once, at a man's gravesite, another woman outcried the man's wife. It was obvious his wife, family, and friends knew who she was, and nothing was said. The wife quickly exited the cemetery chapel and got into the waiting limousine. My heart broke for her!

Families don't always know cemetery protocol. As I was conducting the committal, the husband of the deceased called out, "Preacher, I have a few things I want to say before you get started." His wife's service had been the day before, so I was familiar with his interruptions. He gave his final goodbyes to her and thanked the family while giving me a look letting me know I could proceed.

As the preacher, you cannot be so tied to tradition you don't allow families to have their final say.

> **1 Thessalonians 4:14-17** For since we believe that Jesus died and rose again, even so, through Jesus, God will bring with him those who have fallen asleep.
>
> [15]For this we declare to you by a word from the Lord, that we who are alive, who are left until the coming of the Lord, will not precede those who have fallen asleep.
>
> [16]For the Lord himself will descend from heaven with a cry of command, with the voice of an archangel, and with the sound of the trumpet of God. And the dead in Christ will rise first.
>
> [17]Then we who are alive, who are left, will be caught up together with them in the clouds to meet the Lord in the air, and so we will always be with the Lord.

CHAPTER

14

The Repast

Historically, the repast has always been an integral part of many African American communities. Family and friends bring food over long before the service. Fried chicken, ham, ribs, potato salad, macaroni and cheese, sweet potato pie, pound cake, sweet tea, rolls, and soda would be taken to the family home to assist them in feeding everyone who stopped by to visit or traveled a distance for the service. On the day of the service, the sisters are in the kitchen cooking up some food—fried chicken, ham, green beans, fried corn, corn pudding, macaroni and cheese, and potato salad. Never look for a fresh green salad no, no, everything is prepared with love for the family. Every dessert you could imagine shows up, freshly baked by someone at the church. Yes, everything is delicious. It is a way of showing love and respect to the family and the deceased.

At the repast, the most common menu items are fried chicken, mashed potatoes, green beans, roll, iced tea, and dessert (pound cake, yellow cake with chocolate icing, sweet potato pie). What can happen at a repast? Well for one, strained family relationships are on display. Sometimes animosity raises its ugly head between the mother of the deceased child and the child's stepmother. There are times when the key spouse or other family members refuse to return for the repast for fear of an ugly scene.

I have experienced the repast where family members and friends who did not attend the service are invited to come and eat. Everyone is served their meal and suddenly folks start appearing out of nowhere, ready to eat. What does the church do? We feed them without question. Why? Here is another opportunity to show the love of God.

At the repast, we must continue to walk in the love of Jesus. We always take notice of those who are unable to stand in line to receive their food due to disability or age.

The Repast Team is so wonderful at ensuring that everyone who is incapacitated and/or disabled is served.

Yes, there have been occasions when melees almost started at the repast. Preachers must be careful about sharing their personal knowledge, for they only have one side of the story. After one service, the family was extremely upset about stories shared by the preacher. We had no idea how upset they were until we arrived at the repast. Suddenly, I heard raised voices. Folks started standing up and breaking into groups. I had to raise my voice and say, "Not here." After meeting with the family and the visiting preacher, it became clear what had occurred. Remember every pancake, no matter how flat, has two sides. The preacher only presented one side of the deceased, and the family was offended because he did not tell their side of the story. It was better if he had not shared those one-sided conversations which demeaned others.

More often, the repast ends up being a joyful gathering. Repast often serves as a family reunion, where many pictures are taken, and family stories are rehashed. Conversation can become so pleasant and joyful family members forget they are at the church, and we must announce that the repast has ended.

Repasts are served by volunteers who have been at the church many hours preparing for the family; the volunteers' service is invaluable. Repasts are generally two hours in length from the time the family sits and down and begins to eat.

I am often asked if I eat at the repast. Generally, I don't. Not because the food isn't delicious, but I may have done several homegoing services in the month (or even two in a week), and I just don't have the desire for the food. However, I appreciate the fact the food is available.

Philippians 2:1-5 So if there is any encouragement in Christ, any comfort from love, any participation in the Spirit, any affection and sympathy,

²Complete my joy by being of the same mind, having the same love, being in full accord and of one mind.

³Do nothing from rivalry or conceit, but in humility count others more significant than yourselves.

⁴Let each of you look not only to his own interests, but also to the interests of others.

⁵Have this mind among yourselves, which is yours in Christ Jesus

❊ ❊ ❊

My Health

Yes, as the eulogist I cry. I have cried at the start of the eulogy, and God strengthens so I can stand. I have eulogized friends, those who I have laughed and traveled with, and when I stand, my heart aches. I don't try to hold back my tears, but I do ask the Lord to compose me. I can hear Reverend A. Colette Rice or Minister James Durham calling out to me "preach, preacher."

People often ask me "How do you do it? How do you preach all those eulogies week after week? I couldn't do it!" I smile and let them know I stand because the Spirit of God stands up inside me and pushes me upward to my feet. I preach because God has called me to preach. This is the place He has assigned me, and I am thankful for the opportunity to be used by God.

However, I have learned the importance of taking time for myself. I tried learning to play the piano…which did not work out very well. Then, I learned how to make jewelry and completely lost myself in the creation and construction of each piece. I thank God for giving me this gift.

I also started a nonprofit organization with several components. One component is dedicated to serving the underserved and the disenfranchised throughout the metropolitan area of Washington, DC (including Maryland and Virginia). I am thankful for the opportunity to host a book bag drive, giving out 350 book bags stuffed with school supplies. During Thanksgiving and Christmas, we serve hot meals to senior citizens. The other component of my nonprofit is a talk show, *Generationally Speaking*. The show features me and two other hosts, Pastor Sha'Meca Latai Oliver (founder of Women Who Lead Connect) and Minister James Durham (Associate Pastor at Mt. Ennon Baptist Church). Our conversations are always lively, as we discuss life issues and struggles through our distinct perspectives. The show can be viewed every Wednesday night at 9:30 pm on TheNowNetwork.org or on my YouTube Channel *Generationally Speaking*. It has been an exhilarating experience hearing the perspective of the younger generation.

I must admit trying to introduce exercise into my day has been a crawl, walk, stumble, and a "get back up." The pool provides the best method of exercise for me since it is easier on my joints.

Not only is my physical health important but so is my mental health. I have learned how to release the weight of the conversation I just had with a family who has experienced loss; I call on God to help me. I surrender it all to him. Writing this book has been good for my soul!

CHAPTER

16

In Closing

Just like I hated going to the hospital for a season, I also disliked going to the cemetery. The thought of leaving your loved one out there, in a dark hole, inside a closed box was too much for me to think about. I remember a service at a military cemetery. Once I'd finished the committal, I looked over and saw the casket sitting atop a stone structure, ready for burial. It seemed incomplete and it broke my heart.

However, I have learned that God knows every word, thought, and action in my spirit. God knew my heart's turmoil, and He provided an answer. I hear from God most often when my spirit is at rest. When everything around me is quiet, He speaks to my spirit. It was in such a quiet moment God gave me the comfort and answer to my travail. He said, "Irene, what is being deposited into the ground is simply the shell which held the person. The essence of who they were, their spirit, their soul has taken flight on the very day I called them home to me." I was released and began to experience the cemetery more positively.

Funeral after funeral, the various causes of death can be overwhelming. In another conversation with God, He reminded me, "I called you to preach, and this is the last official service to be offered; give the family your best and I will supply you with the words to say." He has never come short of His promise. I remain amazed at how the messages always provide what the family needed to hear.

Funeral after funeral, I pray for words of comfort to give each family. I have tried to rehash previous sermons, however, it just never seemed to work for me. I have not become numb to preaching eulogies, and I don't view them as just another service. Each time, the Spirit of God reminds me this is a family who is experiencing the transition of a mother, a father, a husband, a wife, or a child or a family member who is experiencing the death of a loved one for the first time. Everyone on the team has the same mantra: "give our very best." We have collectively learned when we support each other in our respective roles everything flows better for the family and for us as a team.

In closing, I am thankful to my Pastor, Dr. Delman Coates for having confidence in me to handle this sensitive assignment—to stand, representing the church, and preach what thus saith the Lord.

I pray this book will be a source of joy, one you can share with family and friends. I hope together you can rejoice in the knowledge "Some glad morning when this life is over, we will fly away to be with our loved ones, and more importantly, with our Lord Jesus the Christ." However, remember every tomorrow is "Some glad morning" an opportunity for you to enjoy life, to give back, to rejoice and be glad in it.

Revelation 21:1-7 Then I saw "a new heaven and a new earth," for the first heaven and the first earth had passed away, and there was no longer any sea.

[2] I saw the Holy City, the new Jerusalem, coming down out of heaven from God, prepared as a bride beautifully dressed for her husband.

³ And I heard a loud voice from the throne saying, "Look! God's dwelling place is now among the people, and he will dwell with them. They will be his people, and God himself will be with them and be their God.

⁴ 'He will wipe every tear from their eyes. There will be no more death' or mourning or crying or pain, for the old order of things has passed away."

⁵ He who was seated on the throne said, "I am making everything new!" Then he said, "Write this down, for these words are trustworthy and true."

⁶ He said to me: "It is done. I am the Alpha and the Omega, the Beginning and the End. To the thirsty I will give water without cost from the spring of the water of life.

⁷ Those who are victorious will inherit all this, and I will be their God and they will be my children.

9 781737 832454